Sophie & The German Magician

At The Fair

One day Sophie went to a fair with her parents and her sister Maya and they saw a German magician.

The magician greeted everyone with "**Hallo!**" This means hello in German. Then he said in German that his name was Lukas.

For his first trick, the German magician put three boxes on a table. He placed a coin in one of the boxes. He then told everyone to clap and count to three in German. And if you are reading this story now then please join in too as the magician needs as much help as possible:

eins   zwei   drei

Then they all had to guess which box the coin was in!

Sophie watched in amazement. It wasn't in **eins**. It wasn't in **zwei**. And it *wasn't* in **drei**!

The coin had disappeared!

For his next trick, he asked everyone to clap and say three times **ein Kaninchen**.

Ein Kaninchen   ein Kaninchen   ein Kaninchen.

Sophie's mum whispered to her that **ein Kaninchen** was the German word for a rabbit. And then suddenly out of his hat came……

ein Kaninchen

Next the German magician got out his wand. He told everyone to clap and say three times **ein Vogel**.

Sophie's mum whispered to her that **ein Vogel** was the German word for a bird.

Suddenly **ein Vogel** appeared on the table!

How had he done that? It was amazing!

Next he turned to Sophie and he asked:

"Was ist dein Lieblingstier?"

"Ich mag Hunde."

Sophie realised that Lieblingstier meant favourite animal. So she replied **ich mag Hunde** as she liked dogs. Surely he couldn't make a dog appear!

This time, he had a very long balloon in his hand. He asked the crowd to join in with him as he said:

Ein Hund   ein Hund   **ein Hund**.

And then suddenly the balloon turned into….

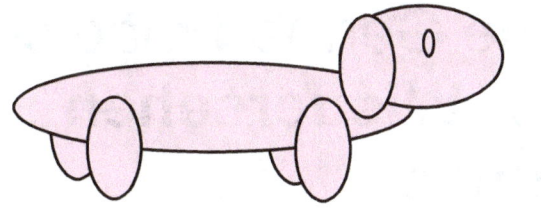

ein Hund

It had been so much fun watching the German magician! For his final trick he placed his hat on the floor and he asked everyone to say **Süßigkeiten** three times as they clapped:

And out of the hat came some **Süßigkeiten** - lots and lots of delicious looking sweets! That was really amazing! Everyone thanked the magician by saying "**Danke**." That was the German magician's last trick, so they all said "**Auf Wiedersehen**". That means goodbye in German.

Sophie & The German Magician

Sophie's Birthday Party

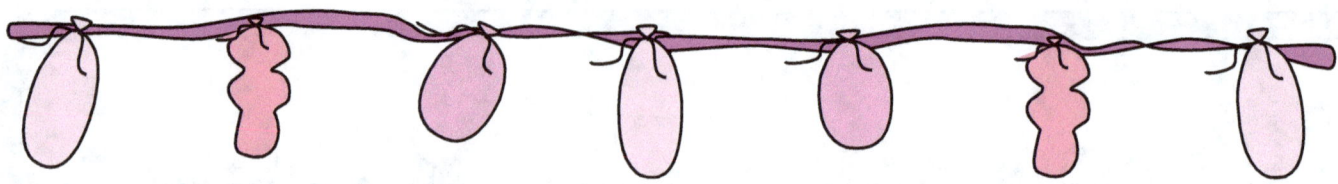

It was Sophie's birthday, and the German magician arrived at her birthday party!

> Hallo!
> Ich heiße Lukas.

The German magician said hello in German. Then he said that his name was Lukas.

Sophie introduced herself in German to the German magician.

> Hallo!
> Ich heiße Sophie.

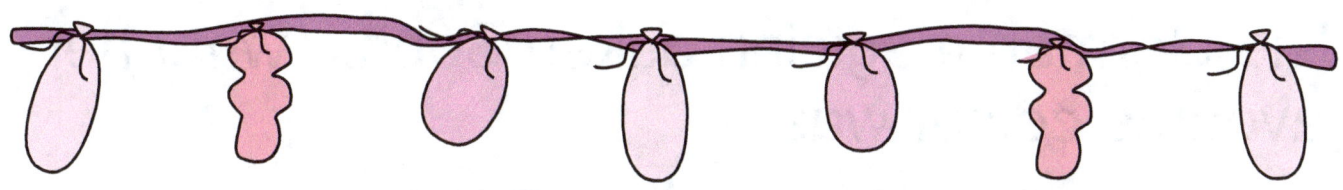

The German magician asked Sophie how she was:

> Wie geht's?

Sophie was feeling **very good** as it was her birthday party! So she replied:

> Sehr gut.

The German magician asked Sophie what her favourite colour was.

Was ist deine Lieblingsfarbe?

Rosa.

Sophie's favourite colour was pink, so she said **rosa**. Pink in German is **rosa**.

Okay, boys and girls I need your help!
We need to say **rosa** three times as we clap.

(Now the magician needs as much help as possible, so if you're reading this story now, please join in too!)

Rosa   rosa   rosa.

And out of the hat came a teddy that was the colour….

Sophie was so happy that she thanked the magician in German.

Next the magician turned to Maya, and he asked:

Maya said blue was her favourite colour.

Okay, boys and girls I need your help!
We need to say **blau** three times as we clap.

(Now the magician needs as much help as possible, so if you're reading this story now, please join in too!)

Blau   blau   blau.

And out of the hat came a teddy that was the colour….

blau

Maya was so happy that she thanked the magician in German.

Next the German magician asked a boy:

Was ist deine Lieblingsfarbe?

Grün.

The boy said green was his favourite colour.

Okay, boys and girls I need your help!
We need to say **grün** three times as we clap.

(Now the magician needs as much help as possible, so if you're reading this story now, please join in too!)

Grün   grün   grün.

And out of the hat came a teddy that was the colour….

Wow, what a magician!

Out of the hat kept on coming more and more teddies for Sophie's friends!

Eventually EVERYONE had a new teddy!

Can you remember the colours in German for all the new teddies?   Lets say them together!

It had been a wonderful birthday party! The German magician waved goodbye and they all said "**Auf Wiedersehen**."

© Joanne Leyland 2023

The useful German words and phrases and the song lyrics may be photocopied by the purchasing individual or institution for use in class or at home.   The rest of the book may not be photocopied or reproduced digitally without the prior written agreement of the author.

Useful German words and phrases

Hallo.. Hello

Ich heiße... My name is …

Wie geht's?... How are you?

Sehr gut .... Very well

Danke... Thank you

Auf Wiedersehen .... Goodbye

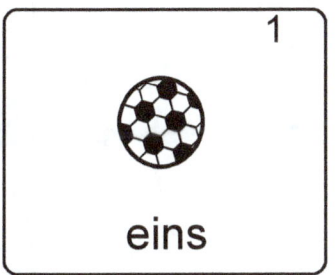 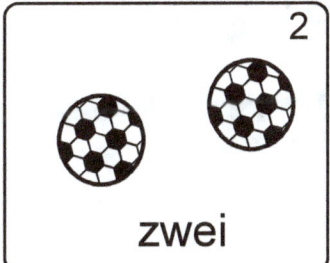 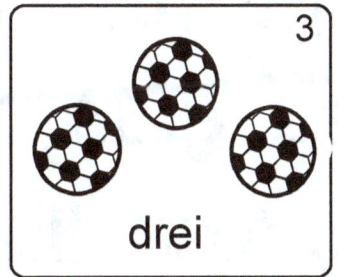 

Was ist dein Lieblingstier? ....What is your favourite animal?

Was ist deine Lieblingsfarbe?.....What is your favourite colour?

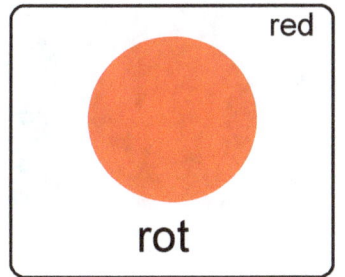 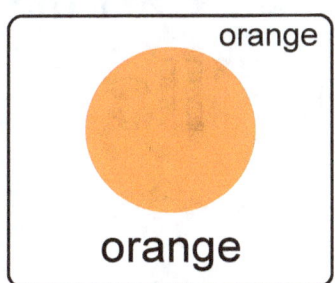 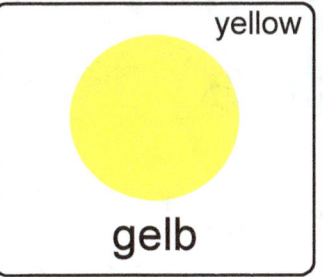 

 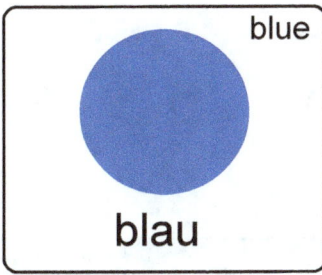  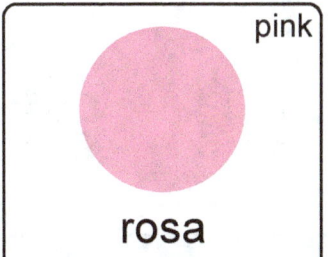

© Joanne Leyland - This page may be photocopied by the purchasing individual or institution for use in class or at home

Let's sing a song!

The following words could either be sung to a made up tune, or you could try saying the words as a rap.

For inspiration of a melody to use you could hum first a nursery rhyme. How many different versions can you create using the lyrics?

rot orange, rot orange
grün blau, grün blau
rosa lila, rosa lila
gelb, gelb

rot orange, rot orange
grün blau, grün blau
rosa lila, rosa lila
gelb, gelb